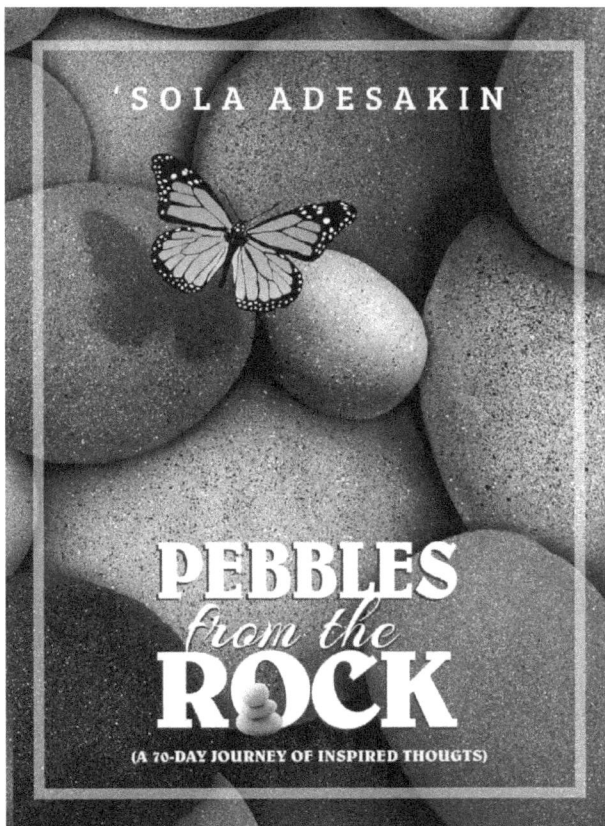

'SOLA ADESAKIN

PEBBLES
from the
ROCK

(A 70-DAY JOURNEY OF INSPIRED THOUGTS)

Pebbles from the Rock

Copyright © 2016 by Sola Adesakin

Paperback ISBN: 978-978-945-757-1

Published by: FRUIT Foundation
Email: info@fruitfoundation.org

Cover Design: Deji Akinpelu
Email: akintee79@yahoo.com

Interior Design& Editing: Temitope Adewale
Email: info@dewalette.com

Printed in the United States of America.

CONTENT

Dedication

*To God the Father, who has created us in
His image; He is the One who gives
Inspiration to men.*

*To God the Son, who has made known to us
the mystery of the love of God.*

*To God the Spirit, who continually
opens our eyes of understanding to
behold our inheritance in the saints.*

Acknowledgment

I honor all my ministry helpers and friends; too numerous to mention, Thank you for believing in me.

I appreciate my Spiritual Parents and Mentors in faith for their prayers, encouragement and support. I'm glad to be in a generation of great men and women with exploits parallel to and greater than what I read in the Bible. Jesus said it already–Greater works shall you do.

I specially acknowledge Rev Funke Felix-Adejumo, Pastor Nike Adeyemi, Pastor Mayokun Oreofe and Pastor Dotun Arifalo.

Grateful to my biological parents Pa Mosudi and Mrs Ebunoluwa Olukokun: I honour you; Heaven won't stop paying you for your sacrifice of love. To all of my siblings, God's love keeps binding us together.

To my Husband and Número-Uno Cheerleader; Adegboyega, a rare kind of man, I celebrate you! And to the three amazing guys that call me Mama, you are trees of righteousness and plantings in the Lord's house.

I appreciate Temitope Adewale of Dewalette Creations and Claire Oluwatoyin Abdul-Azeez for their efforts on this book.

Destiny is here!

1

SHINE IN THE MIDST OF DARKNESS!

*In the beginning God created the heavens and the earth. [2] The
earth was without form, and void; and darkness was on the face of
the deep. And the Spirit of God was hovering over the face of the
waters.[3] Then God said, "Let there be light"; and there was light.
[4] And God saw the light that it was good; and God divided the
light from the darkness. [5] God called the light Day,
and the darkness He called Night* (Genesis 1: 1-5)

Reading Genesis 1 all over again, my conclusion
is that God is infinitely perfect! He saw darkness and
commanded light out of it. He didn't banish the
darkness entirely; there needed to be night seasons
because His creation (man especially) would need to
sleep and rest. If all we had was Day, we would be
worn out because there wouldn't be an opportunity
to sleep and recuperate from our daily activities.

Your night seasons are all part of God's
orchestration; He needs you to rest and sleep in Him
when it's all quiet and dark. Weeping MAY endure
for the night...Joy WILL come in the morning...

My Father, help me to rest in You even when it seems like all is quiet and dark because You are working all things out in my favour, in Jesus' name.

_____

_____

_____

_____

_____

_____

_____

_____

_____

_____

_____

2

FOCUS IN FLOW

There is no one greater in this house than I, nor has he kept back anything from me but you, because you are his wife. How then can I do this great wickedness, and sin against God?" (Genesis 39:9)

If Joseph had given in to the temptation from Potiphar's wife, at the most, he would have become the Prime Messenger of Mrs Potiphar's household. Instead of giving in to the temptation, He looked at the big picture; he knew there was a future ahead; he held on to his dreams and he fled all appearances of evil. He, therefore, became the Prime Minister of a nation.

Focus is key if we want to achieve the best in life. Temptations look attractive in the immediate, but their consequences are every expensive in the long run. Sin is sin, no matter how small.

I receive the grace to resist temptations. I will stay on God's course for my life. I will not give in to the enticement of the evil one in Jesus' name.

_____

_____

_____

_____

_____

_____

_____

_____

_____

_____

_____

_____

3

GOD'S WAY; THE WAY

And He said to them, "Cast the net on the right side of the boat, and you will find some." So they cast, and now they were not able to draw it in because of the multitude of fish.
(John 21:6)

The first time Jesus performed a miracle for Peter and his co-fishermen, Jesus told them to cast their nets into the DEEP and they caught so many fish that their net began to break. The second time they saw such a miracle, Jesus told them to cast their net into the RIGHT SIDE of the sea; they did and caught so many BIG fish, but their net did not break.

God reveals Himself to us again and again and how He does, or how our miracles happen, is not for us to figure out. What is most important is that we OBEY and exercise our faith. I see your net breaking with overflowing provision.

Father, help me to obey your instructions, no matter how strange they may be to me. As I exercise my faith in obeying you, I will experience miracles in Jesus' name.

_____

_____

_____

_____

_____

_____

_____

_____

_____

_____

_____

_____

4

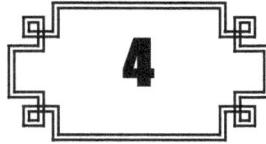

PUMPED FOR PURPOSE

"Before I formed you in the womb I knew you;
Before you were born I sanctified you;
I ordained you a prophet to the nations." (Jer. 1:5)

Every scene in a movie script is deliberate and specifically chosen to add to the essence of the movie. God is our Scriptwriter. He has chosen exactly what will add up—the cast, the cost, the costume, the props and the locations. In the movie of your life, enjoy the series, the scenes, the action and the somber moments. Trust the Master Producer for every scene you have to act in.

Experience has shown that God does only Masterpieces; His stories are always Divine-Oscar winning. Remove the Prison from Joseph's story, and he might never have met Pharaoh. Remove his brothers' envy, and he might never have gotten to Egypt. Now act your life-story in elegance and with sophistication; trusting your Producer absolutely!

Father, as you take me through the different scenes in life,
help me to trust You because You have everything in place to
make a beautiful and joyous ending out of my life.

_____

_____

_____

_____

_____

_____

_____

_____

_____

_____

_____

_____

5

UP ON HIS BACK; BACKED UP BY HIM

And he said, "I have been very zealous for the Lord God of hosts; because the children of Israel have forsaken Your covenant, torn down Your altars, and killed Your prophets with the sword. I alone am left; and they seek to take my life (1 Kings 19:14)

Elijah, the great prophet, got overwhelmed at some point and He told God he was the only one standing for Him. God shocked him by saying there were 7,000 men who were reserved and hadn't defiled themselves! The moral of that story is that God has multiple options for each person. If you are not fulfilling God's purpose for your life, you may be replaced (Remember Saul and David).

No doubt, life may be sometimes very inundating and you just want to throw in the towel, but find Joy in your Journey, Ministry in your Mystery and Comfort in your Conflicts. The bible says no temptation has taken you which is uncommon to man (1st Cor. 10:13). Faithful is He who has called you, who also will do it.

I will fulfill the purpose of God for my life. I will not give up in the face of any obstacle in my path to destiny. I will not be replaced in Jesus' name.

_____

_____

_____

_____

_____

_____

_____

_____

_____

_____

_____

_____

6

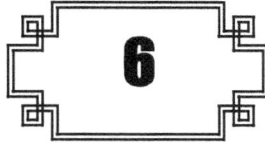

YOU CAN'T BE ALONE

God sets the solitary in families; He brings out those who are
bound into prosperity; But the rebellious dwell in a dry land.
(Psalm 68:6)

He grants the barren woman a home,
Like a joyful mother of children.
Praise the Lord! (Psalm 113:9)

God loves companionship- "Let us make man in our image" (Gen 1:26); "He keeps the solitary in families" (Psa 68:6); "None shall lack her mate" (Isa 34:16); "Be fruitful and multiply" (Gen 1:28); "He makes the barren keep house" (Psa 113:9).

These and many other scriptures reveal the intentions of God for His children on earth. Feeling lonely and left out? He's very much on your case......
He's working it out. Trust Him

Father, Your promise to me is that You will never leave me nor forsake me. I believe that You are working things out and bringing the right company my way.

_____

_____

_____

_____

_____

_____

_____

_____

_____

_____

_____

_____

7

DO YOU SPILL PEOPLE'S SECRETS?

The secret of the Lord is with those who fear Him, And He will show them His covenant. (Psalm 24:14)

Everyone has secrets; even God. The bible says He keeps His secrets with those who fear Him. When a person shares issues of their life with you in confidence, it's a privilege. Unauthorized and unnecessary spillage of that information is sacrilege; before God and Man.

How have you fared in keeping people's secrets? Do you share them as prayer points with an ulterior motive of divulging the info or can you be trusted?

I receive the grace to be a good custodian of secrets. When people share their story with me, I will count it as a privilege and be a good steward.

_____

_____

_____

_____

_____

_____

_____

_____

_____

_____

_____

_____

8

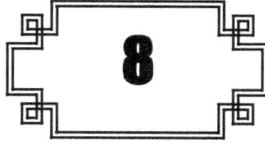

THIS OBEDIENCE; NOT DISOBEDIENCE

*He said to him, "I too am a prophet as you are, and an angel spoke to me by the word of the L*ord*, saying, 'Bring him back with you to your house, that he may eat bread and drink water.' " (He was lying to him.)* (1 Kings 13:18)

The prophet in this scripture disobeyed God and obeyed a senior prophet instead and he lost his life in the process. Peter out of genuine concern, took Jesus aside and tried to persuade him from the vision of the cross for which the salvation of the entire universe was dependent! But Jesus answered him accordingly.

Many times people are more "concerned"(genuinely) for you than God Himself is and they give you ungodly counsel or try to persuade you away from what is God's will. There's no need to fight anyone. Politely ignore them, firmly insist on what God has told you, and run with your vision. Tell them, "I will make it." The key to your achievement is not in the hands of any human being!

Father, please give me wisdom to differentiate between right and wrong counsels. I receive the grace to say NO to anything against Your will for my life.

_____

_____

_____

_____

_____

_____

_____

_____

_____

_____

_____

_____

9

FAST TRACK TO DESTINY

I returned and saw under the sun that—The race is not to the swift, Nor the battle to the strong, Nor bread to the wise, Nor riches to men of understanding, Nor favor to men of skill; But time and chance happen to them all. (Ecclesiastes 9:11)

That your pace in life is slower than that of others does not mean your destiny is lower; ask Joseph. That you have a delay in an area does not mean you will come last in the relay of life; ask Abraham, Sarah, Hannah and Elizabeth. Finally, that you stumble on one or more occasions does not mean you will fumble in life; ask David.

God rules in the affairs of men and He has the blueprint for your life. In one day, God transformed a "certain" son of Jesse into a household and eternally celebrated name called David. Something from Nothing; Someone from Nobody, Nothing beats Divine Metamorphosis. God is the time and chance that happens to what Strength and Swiftness can't achieve.

*Father, set me on high by Your mighty power. End
every unnecessary delay and put me on a fast track to
my destiny in Jesus' name.*

_____

_____

_____

_____

_____

_____

_____

_____

_____

_____

_____

_____

10

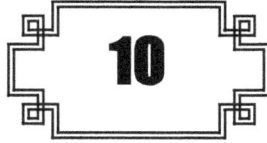

FROM REJECTION TO ELECTION

So now, go. I am sending you to Pharaoh to bring my people
the Israelites out of Egypt." (Exodus 3:10)

Moses had the best upbringing while growing up in the palace, but at some point when he wanted to help his brethren, he was rejected and they asked him who made him a ruler and judge over them. This led to his being ejected from the Palace and sentenced to the Wilderness. After 40 years, this same Moses became a ruler and judge over his people.

You may have been rejected but please don't be dejected. When God is in the picture, you are Connected, Protected, Respected and you will yet be selected. Where you have been rejected, you will yet be Re-elected and your appointment will be visible for all to see. Cheer Up!

Father, just like You changed Moses' story, intervene in my life and turn every rejection to a glorious appointment in Jesus' name.

_ _

_ _

_ _

_ _

_ _

_ _

_ _

_ _

_ _

_ _

_ _

_ _

11

A VOICE TO REJOICE

*Then the women said to Naomi, "Blessed be the Lord, who
has not left you this day without a close relative; and may his
name be famous in Israel!* (Ruth 4:14)

When my neighbor gets a blessing, it shows God
is in my neighborhood. When my friend testifies, it
means God is around my end. When my brother is
dazzled by God's goodness, I dance because it means
my blessing is nearer and when my sister starts to
narrate how God has visited her, I rejoice because it
is proof my turn is here.

Wait a minute, what's your reaction when someone
around you testifies of God's goodness? When Ruth
is blessed, Naomi enjoys of the overflow.
Partake of someone's joy today and yours will come
tumbling in. A testimony is proof that tests do end.

By Your grace, Lord, I rejoice with those who rejoice even when I'm still expecting my miracle. I will soon share my testimony in Jesus' name.

_____

_____

_____

_____

_____

_____

_____

_____

_____

_____

_____

_____

12

ELEGANCE THROUGH DILIGENCE

Do you see a man who excels in his
work? He will stand before kings;
He will not stand before unknown men. (Prov 22:29)

Some are made famous by the greatness of their fathers (like Solomon who inherited so much as a king); some make their fathers famous by their achievements (the world would not have known Jesse if not for David). Whichever way, enduring success is deliberate and worked for.

It doesn't matter if you were born with a silver spoon or not, you can turn back the hands of time and decide to eat with silver, gold, platinum spoons all your life! Start now. Be diligent in your work. Aim high and you will get to the top.

Despite my history, I dedicate myself to diligence and by the grace of God, I will attain great heights in Jesus' name.

13

BRILLIANTLY SIGNIFICANT

*But the Lord said to Samuel, "Do not look at his appearance
or at his physical stature, because I have refused him. For the
Lord does not see as man sees; for man looks at the outward
appearance, but the Lord looks at the heart."*
(1 Samuel 16:7)

In the game of football, the spotlight is usually on
the players. However, there's someone important
in the match who may be inconspicuous but holds
a very important role. He can decide to fire any of
the players for a good reason and he can stop the
match if need be—the Referee!

What you are doing now may look insignificant;
you may think you do not matter to the world but
I can assure you that in God's eyes, you are too
precious to be left out of the game of life. When
the devil taunts you with your past or threatens
your destiny, remind him of his future—eternal
condemnation. He is doomed for eternity but
boom! You will shine eternally with Christ!

God, help me realize that You have the final say in my life. Whatever my hands find to do, no matter how small it may seem, it shall greatly prosper in Jesus' name.

_____

_____

_____

_____

_____

_____

_____

_____

_____

_____

_____

_____

14

TEARY? TARRY!

*That you do not become sluggish, but imitate those who through
faith and patience inherit the promises.*
(Hebrews 6:12)

Zacharias and his wife prayed for many years for
a child but they were oblivious to the fact that the
child they would bear had been pre-destined to
come exactly six (6) months before Jesus would
come through Mary. They kept praying, attending
services, giving and serving and when the time
came, an angel appeared to Zacharias at the place
of service.

With God involved in a plan, delay is non-existent.
Everything is working just according to plan. If
you will hold on long enough, answers to your
prayers will come and will be obvious for all to see.
You are going to birth something that will be
trans-generational. Hold on!

Father, I receive the patience to hold on till I see the manifestation of Your promises to me. They will come to pass because You cannot lie.

_____

_____

_____

_____

_____

_____

_____

_____

_____

_____

_____

_____

_____

15

MELODY AFTER JEOPARDY

For our light, momentary affliction (this slight distress of the passing hour) is ever more and more abundantly preparing and producing and achieving for us an everlasting weight of glory [beyond all measure, excessively surpassing all comparisons and all calculations, a vast and transcendent glory and blessedness never to cease!] (2 Cor 4:17, Amplified)

When you think life is too hard; think NAOMI.

She lost her husband and 10 years after, her two married sons died. Was it a coincidence that none of them gave her a grandchild? How could both of them have died about the same time? How could both daughters-in-law be barren? Call it Double, Triple Jeopardy! But God wasn't done with her.

Fast forward a couple of years; she became the great-grandmother to David. Call it Divine Restoration, Compensation, Beautification. In your life, God knows what HE is doing, He's aware of the happenings. Can you trust HIM enough?

Father, I consecrate myself to You. Refine me and let me come out as pure gold.

GAIN FROM PAIN

But may the God of all grace, who called us to His eternal
glory by Christ Jesus, after you have suffered a while,
perfect, establish, strengthen, and settle you. (1 Cor. 5:10)

Bathsheba was a woman who knew pain. From
the pain of adultery, to the agony of losing her
husband, to being castigated by the entire community
and finally to losing the first child she had with David
(that might have been her first child ever). In spite of
all, God still honored her. Through her womb came
the wealthiest and wisest king of the earth. In 1 Kings
2:19, Solomon rose to honor her and she sat by his
right hand.

It doesn't matter what you've been through or
what you are going through. When you are in
God's plan, your life can't be plain—you will reign
in spite of your pain...Rejoice.

In the name of Jesus, all my pain will be turned to gain.
Father, lift me far above every unpleasant circumstance I
have come across.

_____

_____

_____

_____

_____

_____

_____

_____

_____

_____

_____

_____

_____

17

FROM THE REFINER'S MINE

He will sit as a refiner and a purifier of silver;
He will purify the sons of Levi,
And purge them as gold and silver,
That they may offer to the Lord
An offering in righteousness. (Malachi 3:3)

Therefore thus says the LORD of hosts: "Behold, I will refine
them and test them, for what else can I do, because of my
people? (Jeremiah 9:7)

In this age of digital photos and wait-and-get pictures, we are gradually forgetting the days when negatives of photographs were developed in the dark room. A lot of us want to have our desires met without God touching our character.

To feature in a future God has given you a picture of, be patient as He develops the negatives in the dark room. As He does, the chaff is taken away from your life and you shine like the STARS. God-inspired and developed pictures make a good future.

My Purifier, as You develop the good picture of my life,
help me to co-operate with You to build godly character.
Take away the chaff, so I can shine like the stars.

_____

_____

_____

_____

_____

_____

_____

_____

_____

_____

_____

_____

_____

18

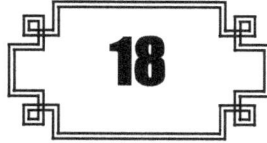

A PERFECT BLUEPRINT

Then I said, "Behold, I come;
In the scroll of the book it is written of me.
⁸I delight to do Your will, O my God,
And Your law is within my heart." (Psalm 40:7-8)

God has the original blueprint for your life. The devil may make an attempt at re-writing your story by introducing loads of unpleasant circumstances. He may try to distort things, but the good news is that God already published your book before you existed. Unknown to the devil, all his tactics have been taken into account and sorted out in the Book.

Something is certain about you: you are definitely going to have a good landing. Before you existed and till eternity, your life is a successfully completed bestselling story! Hallelujah!

*The original blueprint for my life will be fulfilled
whether the devil likes it or not. My beautiful story must
emerge in Jesus' name.*

_____

_____

_____

_____

_____

_____

_____

_____

_____

_____

_____

_____

19

FORMED TO PERFORM

Did You not pour me out like milk,
And curdle me like cheese,
¹¹Clothe me with skin and flesh,
And knit me together with bones and sinews?
¹²You have granted me life and favor,
And Your care has preserved my spirit. (Job 10:10-12)

Whilst in the womb, a baby undergoes a lot of metamorphosis. From the moments of looking like nothing, to the times of webbed fingers, a blurry facial look and eyes firmly shut, up until the time of perfection and beauty, no one understands how these things are fully formed. God is best at work sometimes when you don't "understand". Trust Him enough with your life. If He brought you through the womb; a place of absolute dependence on Him (even your mother couldn't have protected you enough), He will bring you through the womb of every fiery trial. In quietness and confidence shall be your strength (Isa 30:15).

Even when I don't understand how things will work
out, help me to trust in you Lord.

_____

_____

_____

_____

_____

_____

_____

_____

_____

_____

_____

_____

20

CONCEIVE TO ACHIEVE

And He said, "The kingdom of God is as if a man should scatter seed on the ground, and should sleep by night and rise by day, and the seed should sprout and grow, he himself does not know how. For the earth yields crops by itself: first the blade, then the head, after that the full grain in the head.
(Mark 4:26-28)

It is completely futile for someone who is 2 months pregnant to envy another woman who is 9 months pregnant and about to deliver or someone who has just delivered a baby. It is good to wish for another man's result but remember: Life is a Process.

There is a process for every progress to be made and timing for the fruition of every vision, idea and dream. So at whatever stage you are, as long as you have conceived (a vision, idea, dream), take your journey in stride, for in due time you will also bring forth your own and will deliver safely. Have a safe and fruitful ride!

In the name of Jesus, I am empowered to keep striding on my journey to fulfilled dreams. No matter what comes my way, I will get to the place of fruition.

_ _

_ _

_ _

_ _

_ _

_ _

_ _

_ _

_ _

_ _

_ _

_ _

21

HELP FROM HIS HEM

I will lift up my eyes to the hills—
From whence comes my help?
My help comes from the Lord,
Who made heaven and earth (Psalm 121:1-2)

A man can only give you out of what He has received. When people "try" to "help" sometimes, they end up messing the supposed "helped" up. What God wouldn't do, let it remain undone. And why won't He do it? He will use people of course, but it's better to look to Him and He in turn chooses who to use to help you than looking to man and expecting God to endorse.

Huge promises from men many times go unfulfilled, not because of their doings, but because of the frailty, volatility and limited nature of man. Take heed...

Father, You are the source of my help, not any man.
I look to You alone and I will not be ashamed.

_____

_____

_____

_____

_____

_____

_____

_____

_____

_____

_____

_____

22

HE MEETS THE NEEDS OF MEN

The eyes of all look expectantly to You,
And You give them their food in due
season. You open Your hand
And satisfy the desire of every living thing.
(Psalm 145:15-15)

God conveniently fed millions of Israelites day and night in the wilderness for 40 years and the Bible records that He brought them out with gold and silver and NONE was feeble (broke, sick, barren, unemployed, unmarried) amongst them. (Psalm 105:37). Their clothes did not wear out neither did their feet swell (Deuteronomy 8:4).

Our needs (as much and diverse as they are) can never give God a sleepless night–He doesn't sleep or slumber anyway. He is the God that specializes in meeting the needs of His own. Everyone is on His priority list and right on schedule.

Father, I praise You because You are mindful of me and You know my needs. You are more than able to supply all my needs and I know You will in Jesus' name.

23

JOY TO ENJOY

*My brethren, count it all joy when you fall into various
trials, knowing that the testing of your faith produces patience.*
(James 1:2-3)

Has anyone ever wondered where Daniel was, when his friends (Shadrach, Meshach and Abednego) were being thrown into the fire for not bowing to the image? We know Daniel wouldn't have bowed too. He probably was somewhere in his room worshipping. However, the devil doesn't play hide and seek games with people who go all out to stand for God. He is always on the offensive.

Daniel's own test was waiting ahead of him too. Those who were envious of him ganged up to throw him into the lion's den, but he came out victorious! Count it all joy when you fall into diverse temptations, for none of what has taken you is uncommon to man. Having done all, STAND because you will SHINE!

Father, give me the grace to come out victorious through any test that comes my way. I will not fail in Jesus' name.

24

ENSLAVED BUT SAVED BY GRACE

Then out of them shall proceed thanksgiving
And the voice of those who make merry;
I will multiply them, and they shall not diminish;
I will also glorify them, and they shall not be small.
(Jeremiah 30:19)

Joseph wasn't the only slave sold into Egypt at that time, but we hear nothing of anyone else. When God is involved in your life, you can't end up in oblivion or obscurity. Joseph's brothers wanted to kill him, but because God had a purpose for his life, he couldn't die yet.

Things definitely will rough you up in life. A lot of times, people talk behind your back and sometimes taunt you to your face. Life may seem unfair. Be rest assured; when God is involved, it's not over!

Father, just like You took Joseph from the pit to the palace, lift me up from every pit of disappointment and take me to my glorious position in Jesus' name.

_____

_____

_____

_____

_____

_____

_____

_____

_____

_____

_____

_____

25

POTENT MOMENTS

The steps of a good man are ordered by the Lord,
And He delights in his way.
24 Though he fall, he shall not be utterly cast down;
For the Lord upholds him with His hand.
(Psalm 37:23-24)

Divine Moments are SURE (Simple, Unique, Real and Explosive). One of such moments was when Rebecca met with Abraham's servant and gave him water to drink. Little did she know she was on her way to becoming daughter-in-law to a very important person in the history of humanity - Abraham, the father of faith.

Also, young David left his father's house to run an errand of checking on his brothers at the war front. He never knew His name would be on the lips of every Israelite by the end of that night. Divine moments are available, everywhere, every day. Be sensitive, they appear small and simple but they won't leave you the same.

Father, help me to recognize divine moments that will take me to my place of destiny. Help me not to despise them when they appear too small or simple.

_____

_____

_____

_____

_____

_____

_____

_____

_____

_____

_____

_____

_____

26

A TOWER OF COMFORT; BOWELS OF MERCY

Put on therefore, as the elect of God, holy and beloved,
bowels of mercies, kindness, humbleness of mind, meekness,
longsuffering (Colossians 3:12)

Do you think the little maid who referred Naaman to Prophet Elisha would have remained the same after Naaman got back perfectly healed? She was right in the middle of debilitating moments in her life: A young girl who should be starting off her career was a servant, far away from her people. However, she wasn't bitter against her Master or his wife, she reached out to help.

Take a cue from Daniel, Joseph, David & Esther. Circumstances may appear to be "shutting you in". Never shut your mouth from confessing God's words; never shut your bowels of mercy, and never shut yourself away from people you can help or those who can help you. God has designed it so that in this world, we just have to lean on one another...
And soon, your efforts will pay off!

Father, help me to see beyond my present circumstances. I will always see how I can be a positive influence no matter where I find myself in Jesus' name.

_____

_____

_____

_____

_____

_____

_____

_____

_____

_____

_____

_____

27

TACTFUL ACTS

And Elisha sent a messenger to him, saying, "Go and wash in the Jordan seven times, and your flesh shall be restored to you, and you shall be clean." (2 Kings 5:10)

Some things you have to do sometimes are "below" your dignity but in these things are the secrets to greatness, answers to prayers and keys to the next levels. Naaman had to dip himself in the Jordan with his good clothes on.

"Wash in the pool of Siloam..." March around the walls of Jericho for 7 days..." "Go to the poor widow of Zarephath...." Even God, our God uses the foolish things of the world to confound the wise. Never underestimate the power of little acts...Selah

My Father, I humble myself before You. Help me to
follow Your lead no matter how simple they may seem.
I will reap the results of obedience.

28

NO MORE SHAME BUT FAME

When the Lord brought back the captivity of Zion,
We were like those who dream.
Then our mouth was filled with laughter,
And our tongue with singing.
Then they said among the nations,
"The Lord has done great things for them."
(Psalm 126:1-2)

The Samaritan Woman was so conscious of her lifestyle that she didn't draw water at rush hour in order to avoid interaction with other people. But when she met with Jesus and He told her about her life and the living water, she forgot her self-consciousness, left her pot and ran to tell people, "Come and See". She who had been avoiding people then became an Evangelist and convinced multitudes to come to hear Jesus.

Some encounters never leave people the same way. That very sore area of your life will soon become your core Message. Your dung will become your song and pains of your past will give you a blast into fame.

*Father, change every point of shame around me to
beauty in Jesus' name.*

_____
_____
_____
_____
_____
_____
_____
_____
_____
_____
_____
_____

29

A DAY WITH THE RAY!

That you do not become sluggish, but imitate those who through faith and patience inherit the promise. (Hebrews 6:12)

When Daniel heard about the evil decree that would send anyone who worshiped God into the den of lions, He intensified his prayers, worship, confessions, service to God, etc. He even opened his windows so his detractors could see him on his knees praying to God. He was thrown into the lion's den but by the next morning, his status changed forever; he became a toast of the entire nation.

Keep believing God, keep fighting the good fight of faith for your desires, keep confessing the word tenaciously, fellowshipping with the brethren, serving God passionately...On a particular day, Joseph woke up in the prison and slept in the palace; Hannah woke up barren, but slept pregnant; the woman with the issue of blood woke up sick, but went to bed eternally healed. Who knows...TODAY MIGHT JUST BE YOUR DAY!

Lord, help me to keep striving toward the mark even when my breakthrough doesn't seem close. I know my change is sooner than I can see.

_____

_____

_____

_____

_____

_____

_____

_____

_____

_____

_____

_____

_____

30

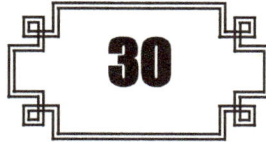

ROOTED IN TRUTH

Behold, I will bring it health and healing; I will heal them and reveal to them the abundance of peace and truth. ⁷And I will cause the captives of Judah and the captives of Israel to return, and will rebuild those places as at the first. (Jer. 22:6-7)

The mouths that said Joseph was dead were the same mouths that said he was alive–thirteen (13) years after. It looked like there would not be respite for him but the God of vindication stepped in.

It might look like the devil (the father of lies) is having an upper hand in your life right now. He might be telling you lies that you are barren, poor, unable to prosper, sick, unqualified, lies embedded in negative medical reports, unfavorable results, etc. The truth of God which is Everlasting will overturn every lie uttered against you and the same people who propagated the lie will proclaim your victory and celebrate you.

Father, I stand upon the truth of Your everlasting word despite the lies of the devil. Every lie of the devil will be swallowed by the performance of Your word in my life.

31

A HERO FROM ZERO

There is therefore now no condemnation to those who are in Christ Jesus, who do not walk according to the flesh, but according to the Spirit. (Roman 8:1)

Moses fled Egypt as a fugitive. He was a murderer who was WANTED. God brought him back as a Hero from zero and he became Israel's greatest deliverer. Nothing was ever mentioned about the murder he had committed. It was only 40 years earlier and even though Pharaoh had died, the reigning Pharaoh never had a record of the murder Moses had committed whilst he lived in the palace. The finger of God had wiped it off the records!

God didn't consult Apostle Paul's past to determine his future. Don't let any devil, person or even you yourself stop you from reaching where God is taking you to! Who is He that condemns? It is God who justifies. When He calls, just say YES LORD.....You have a clean record before Him!

Father, thank You for justifying me and wiping off every negative thing in my past. Because you have qualified me, nobody can decide otherwise. Your say is final.

32

BITTER GUSH TURNED GLITTER RUSH

*Now when they came to Marah, they could not drink the
waters of Marah, for they were bitter. Therefore the name of it
was called Marah. ²⁴And the people complained against
Moses, saying, "What shall we drink?"*
(Exodus 15:23-24)

Marah is just one of the stops in the journey of
life, where it looks like the water is bitter. There is
the Oasis of Elim just at the next stop, where there
are Twelve Springs of Water and Seventy Palm
Trees. Don't despair; don't lose hope, pray to God
and receive His strategy on how to sweeten the
water.

You don't have to endure any situation when it is
apparent that God can turn around the bitterest
and most unpleasant situation into good. Arise,
seek for change and move on to your inheritance;
a place of rest, protection and abundance (Exodus
15:26-27). God, this God still works Wonders!

My God, I thank You because You are a wonder-
working God and there is nothing too hard for you.
Turn every bitter thing in my life to something sweet.

_____

_____

_____

_____

_____

_____

_____

_____

_____

_____

_____

_____

_____

33

ANOINTING ON POINT

For we are His workmanship, created in Christ Jesus for
good works, which God prepared beforehand that we
should walk in them.
(Ephesians 2:10)

When God anoints you, He automatically creates a vacancy for you to occupy even if it did not exist before (consider the stories of David, Joseph, Daniel and Esther).

You don't have to struggle for manifestation. God is not a waster. There's an anointing on you for a reason. This means that as long as His anointing does not stop to flow, there's no end to your shining and progress. Seek His kingdom, His anointing and every other thing shall be added to you.

Father, I thank You that You have prepared a place for me. Let Your anointing continue to flow to me. I shall do exploits in Jesus' name.

34

GOD IS NEVER LATE

While He was still speaking, someone came from the ruler of the synagogue's house, saying to him, "Your daughter is dead. Do not trouble the Teacher." [50]But when Jesus heard it, He answered him, saying, "Do not be afraid; only believe, and she will be made well. (Luke 8:49-50)

God maximizes time, to maximize His glory. Sometimes He waits till it looks like it's over and nothing is going to happen. For Lazarus, it looked like He came late; for Jairus, the Savior didn't need to come anymore because it was "late". Alas our God is the God of the 11th hour miracle, always stepping in a Grand way.

Someone said, "When you realize you can't fix everything, that calms you down and when you know that God can, it cheers you up! Two knockout punches to the devil!"

Father, I thank You because You are not limited by time. It is never too late for You to step in and change any sad story to a happy ending. Father, please step into my situation and turn things around to Your glory in Jesus' name.

_____

_____

_____

_____

_____

_____

_____

_____

_____

_____

_____

_____

35

TENACITY BREAKS THROUGH
HOSTILITY

When you pass through the waters, I will be with you;
And through the rivers, they shall not overflow you.
When you walk through the fire, you shall not be
burned, Nor shall the flame scorch you.
(Isaiah 43:2)

When God was going to promote David, He lifted him from a hostile environment. Esther was once a slave; Joseph passed through the pit, Potiphar's house and the prison; the Israelites went through the wilderness; Hannah was barren and had to live with fruitful Peninnah; Jacob served under greedy Laban; the list of heroes who were once 'zeros' is endless.

The greater the hostility around you, the greater your multiplicity would be; if you don't lose your tenacity. The power of God thrives in the most difficult places and circumstances, just like light thrives and shines well where there is darkness. Don't drown in what you are supposed to be treading on.

Father, You have made me for the top. No matter what
I am going through right now, I know I will emerge
great because You will set me on high.

_____

_____

_____

_____

_____

_____

_____

_____

_____

_____

_____

_____

36

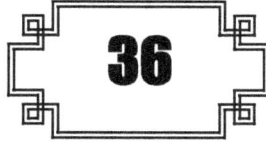

DROPPED BUT NOT STOPPED

The eternal God is your refuge, And
underneath are the everlasting arms;
He will thrust out the enemy from before you,
And will say, 'Destroy!' (Deut 33:27)

Mephibosheth came from the royal line but he was dropped by the person who was supposed to be taking care of Him and he became lame.
God turned his story around and he began to eat at the king's table as one of his sons till he died (2 Sam. 9:7). There are many stories in the Bible about people who were dropped into ugly situations, however, in all of these stories, something was common– they may have been dropped, but underneath were the everlasting arms of the Almighty to sustain them.

When it looks like you have been dropped, it only means you are being borne on Eagles wings (Exodus 19:4) and He can only take you to one place–your place of destiny!

Father, help me to realize that You are carrying me,
even when people disappoint me. You never fail and
You will take me to the finish line.

_____

_____

_____

_____

_____

_____

_____

_____

_____

_____

_____

_____

37

SURRENDER IT ALL TO HIM

Then He got into one of the boats, which was Simon's, and
asked him to put out a little from the land. And He sat
down and taught the multitudes from the boat.
(Luke 5:3)

Peter and the others had left their boats and were washing their nets after a night of toiling and catching not a single fish; they caught NOTHING.

If they were living in days like ours, people might have told them they were cursed. But Jesus came along and got into the empty boat; preaching from it. If the boat had been filled with fish before He came, there probably wouldn't have been space for Him. He finished using their boats and then an abundance of fish surfaced (Luke 5:6-7).

What's the situation around you today? Look at the big picture. It's about time your emptiness gave way to a net-breaking, boat-sinking miracle— just because you yield your all to God.

*My Father, I surrender my life to You. It all belongs
to You. I know You can make something beautiful out
of nothing.*

38

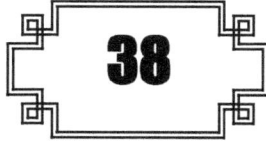

GRATITUDE BRINGS FORTITUDE

Evening and morning and at noon
I will pray, and cry aloud,
And He shall hear my voice.
(Psalm 55:17)

When you make deposits of prayer and praise every morning and every day, you will make withdrawals of blessings all life-long. The name of Jesus is your ATM Card and the Throne of Grace is your ATM machine. This Machine can never run out of resources and the Card can never expire. What a big-breasted God we serve!

God's promises will put you above every oppression, regression, recession and obsession the enemy may be taunting you with. Engage in a session of praise and worship today and pour out an Expression of God's goodness to Him. You are too precious to God to be forgotten. Just like me, you are God's Cinderella; you are His Heroine!

Father, as I praise and worship You, I welcome You into my life once again. Let Your presence consume every evil work in my life, all to your glory in Jesus' name.

_____

_____

_____

_____

_____

_____

_____

_____

_____

_____

_____

_____

_____

39

UNFAILING FAITH; PREVAILING FAITH

"Abraham didn't focus on his own impotence and say, "It's hopeless. This hundred-year-old body could never father a child." Nor did he survey Sarah's decades of infertility and give up. He didn't tiptoe around God's promise asking cautiously skeptical questions. He plunged into the promise and came up strong, ready for God, sure that God would make good on what he had said"
(Romans 4: 19-25, Message)

Do you continually focus on bad news and surrounding circumstances, instead on the word of God? When you start to tiptoe around God's promises and prophecies by asking skeptical questions, you will get cynical human answers and no divine intervention. Plunge deeply (by faith) into God's promises today and stay strong in full assurance; God didn't need assistance to create a beautiful world from absolute chaos (Gen. 1).

In the same way, your desires, challenges and needs can never give Him a headache. Trust Him absolutely! If your faith does not fail, the devil cannot prevail. Having done all, you will testify!

Lord, I receive the grace to ignore negative reports and stay focused on Your promises. My faith will not fail in Jesus' name.

_____

_____

_____

_____

_____

_____

_____

_____

_____

_____

_____

_____

40

VITAL RELATIONSHIPS

He who walks with wise men will be wise,
But the companion of fools will be destroyed.
(Proverbs 13:20)

Relationships are very important in our lives and we must be strategic about them. Sometimes, some relationships are excess luggage (e.g. Lot in Abraham's life, Jonah in the ship going to Tarsus). Some other relationships make your dreams leap (e.g. Mary and Elizabeth), while some make it cheap.

Watch out for your associations. It is always good to walk with people who will sharpen your countenance, not with those who will dampen your spirit. Find those who will alleviate your stress. Nonetheless, sometimes we are to be a source of support to the weak and help them get stronger. Our world would be a better place if we had more genuine and godly relationships such as what existed between Naomi and Ruth–where tribe, past experiences, hurts and disappointments are not a barrier to pouring out into one another.

Father, help me identify godly relationships that will help me on my journey to divine destiny. Give me wisdom to choose my relationships.

_____

_____

_____

_____

_____

_____

_____

_____

_____

_____

_____

_____

_____

41

SAPPED BUT NOT TRAPPED

And Moses was learned in all the wisdom of the Egyptians, and was mighty in words and deeds. (Acts 7:22)

Life's issues are real and sometimes inundating; they sap the strength of a man and make him look helpless and feel worthless. Such was what happened to Moses; a man ordained as the deliverer of God's people. He was living in the Egyptian palace for 40 years and fled to the dessert for another 40 years of his life. So when God appeared to him to tell him he would go deliver the Israelites, he had forgotten his wisdom, strength and eloquence (Acts 7:22). God convinced him into seeing his capabilities and assured him He would be with him.

You see, we are imperfect, susceptible and vulnerable men in the hands of a Sovereign God whose purpose is firm. It doesn't matter where you've been or what people think or what your circumstances say; God is able to marvelously help you till you become strong; and the most beautiful place to be is in God's hands!

*Father, I thank You that I am in Your hands and
despite my past or circumstances, You will make
something beautiful with my life.*

_____

_____

_____

_____

_____

_____

_____

_____

_____

_____

_____

_____

_____

42

STAMPEDE INDEED

And He took off their chariot wheels, so that they drove them with difficulty; and the Egyptians said, "Let us flee from the face of Israel, for the Lord fights for them against the Egyptians."
(Exodus 14:25)

It's either God grants you speed and makes you move super fast or He removes the wheels from the chariots of your enemies and makes them move so slow, rendering them immobile altogether. One thing is certain; they will never catch up with you!

Pharaoh thought the Israelites were defenseless but God proved him wrong. God drowned him and his chariots! It didn't matter how long and how far Saul chased David, David was "untouchable". Going forward, may God make your feet like hinds' feet and set you upon your high places in Jesus name. Amen!

My God, I thank You because my enemies will never catch up with me. You are always fighting for me.

43

WOMAN: LOOSED TO DIFFUSE

But when Jesus saw her, He called her to Him and said
to her, "Woman, you are loosed from your infirmity."
¹³And He laid His hands on her, and immediately she
was made straight, and glorified God.
(Luke 13: 12-13)

Women have always been a subject of the dev-il's attack. Either he wants her head bowed in shame like the woman caught in adultery, or her back bent like the woman with an infirmity of 18 years or her body malfunctioning like the woman with the issue of blood or perhaps make her life chaotic like the woman who had five (5) husbands.

One thing is evident and similar about these women: Jesus had compassion for them. He met all of their needs – psychological, physical, emotional etc. I'm not saying men aren't special, but this is a word for my sister who thinks she's done for and nothing is working anymore. Hear me! Jesus is interested in you, He'll fix you up no matter how bad you things are!

Father, I thank You for Your interest in me. In every way the devil has held me bound, I declare that I am free in Jesus' name.

44

TRACE IT TO GRACE

But by the grace of God I am what I am, and His grace
toward me was not in vain; but I labored more abundantly
than they all, yet not I, but the grace of God which was with
me. (Luke 8:49-50)

Life is in levels and levels are relative. It is needful to know that not everyone moves with you to your next level; they've got their journey too so don't fight them. Moving to a next level requires action - walking, climbing, running, flying, soaring. Just make sure you do not remain at the same point. God's got your back.

The grace you carry will intimidate some and irritate others; some will want to imitate you, some will even hate you and many others will berate you. However, a select few will celebrate you. Grace is innate, your "own" bespoke gift from your Creator. Destiny is too precious to waste time trying to please people or live by their opinion. Celebrate yourself and appreciate the few who celebrate you.

Father, I thank You for your unique which grace You've given me. Please help me to celebrate who You have made me and make impact with what You have given me in Jesus' name.

45

FOLLOW ME FELLOW!

Then He said to another, "Follow Me."
But he said, "Lord, let me first go and bury my father."
⁶⁰Jesus said to him, "Let the dead bury their own dead, but you
go and preach the kingdom of God."
(Luke 9:59-60)

Jesus met with some people who had needs. He performed the miracles they needed and instantly sent them away, beseeching them to tell no one. He probably knew they were not set for the long haul with Him – they were only MMC (Microwave Miracle Christians).On the other hand, Jesus met some other people and told them, "Follow Me".

In fact, a man wanted to follow Him but Jesus, by implication, told him he wasn't welcome, yet immediately after, He told another to follow Him (Luke 9:57). God is not impartial; if you are amongst the few He has chosen to follow him (to be discipled by Him), you are most blessed of all men. It might be a long journey, but it will be worth your while on earth and for eternity. Don't be a miracle seeking fellow only; follow Jesus closely too.

Father, help me to be Your true follower and not merely
a miracle seeker.

_____
_____
_____
_____
_____
_____
_____
_____
_____
_____
_____
_____

46

FULLNESS UNTO RICHNESS

And of His fullness we have all received, and grace for grace
(John 1:16)

Life requires that we make purchases and empty our carts from time to time. I know of the best discount code that makes you pay nothing. It's GRACE. I may not be able to fully explain what Grace is, but I know it means meeting God at every turn. It means when there's a bend, that doesn't mean the end; it means when you think you are down to nothing, God is up to something. It's that surprise that God pulls when you think there's nothing more; when angels literally carry you when you fall; when a delay doesn't mean you will come last in the relay.

I have enjoyed it and so I can talk about it. It's a must-subscribe-for code to cruise through life successfully. Enjoy!

Lord, I subscribe to Your grace; let Your grace carry me through every season of my life.

47

CONFLICTED BUT NOT CONSTRICTED

Many are the afflictions of the righteous,
But the Lord delivers him out of them all.
(Psalm 34:19)

As bees are attracted to the honeycomb, so is Satan keenly attracted to any great destiny. The devil doesn't attack worthless ventures. David was constantly an object of attack, but nothing was ever mentioned about the challenges in his brothers' lives. There may be fiery storms on the way to the "other side", but with Jesus in the boat, safe arrival is guaranteed!

David said in Psalm 57:2, "I will cry out to God Most High, To God who PERFORMS all things for me". You see, the problem is that we want to "perform" and want God to "believe" in our performance. But ours is to just to believe, while His is to perform. Blessed is she who believes for there shall be a performance of that which was spoken to her.

I declare that I am a believer;
My Father is the Performer.

48

BOAZ: A TOPAZ

So Boaz took Ruth and she became his wife; and when he went in to her, the Lord gave her conception, and she bore a son.
(Ruth 4:13)

In Ruth chapter 4, the Kinsman who should have "redeemed" Ruth in addition to the land refused. Redeeming Ruth was a no-no for him; probably because of her past and background.

May God give us men like Boaz who would be willing to see and "acquire" not only the "land and the property" i.e. the good things in a woman but are willing to also take on the seemingly not-too-good areas and nurture them into the best. Men who bring out the best in you; Men who are never intimidated, Men who are not opportunists but are your best cheerleaders; they encourage you to keep going! They don't have to be the spouses; the Boaz-kind of men could be a brother, a colleague, a friend, a boss; Men with good intentions. God will always give such Men Lasting Legacies!

*Father, surround me with good people like Boaz and
help me to be someone's cheerleader in Jesus' name.*

49

ENDOWED TO WOW

Or does He say it altogether for our sakes? For our sakes, no doubt, this is written, that he who plows should plow in hope, and he who threshes in hope should be partaker of his hope.
(1 Corinthians 9:10)

Breast milk is not produced all through a woman's life. It is a supply necessitated by an event and it is for a purpose. Pregnancy triggers this process so that after childbirth, the baby will be fed. In the same way, every endowment of God in your life is for a purpose and there are graces for different seasons. No one is going to be here forever, hence the need to identify your purpose, endowments, lessons and destiny-helpers for every season and maximize them in the most optimal manner.

Put your hands to the plow and keep going; there is grace and help available at the Father's throne. You are divinely endowed to wow your world!

Lord, help me to identify the things You have endowed me with and give me the grace to utilize them optimally. I am a wonder to my world.

50

ATTRACTIVE DISTRACTIONS

*But when He had turned around and looked at His disciples, He
rebuked Peter, saying, "Get behind Me, Satan! For you are not
mindful of the things of God, but the things of men."*
(Mark 8:33)

The men of Issachar were men who had
understanding of times and seasons. They knew
what Israel ought to do at every moment. A lot of
Christians today lack spiritual insight into the
happenings in and around their lives. We ought to be
like Jesus, who by a discerning spirit, rebuked Peter
when the devil was trying to "use" him as a distraction.

There are many distractions screaming for our attention
in the world today and if we give in to them, our
spiritual antenna will be weakened. Wherever there is
anything contrary to the fruit of the Spirit, the devil is
present: that's where you find envy, bitterness,
animosity, gossip, hatred etc. Whatever is not of faith
(righteousness, peace and joy in the Holy Ghost) is sin.
Stay away from distractions, no matter how attractive
they look.

Confession: I receive the grace to say no to any distraction
on my path to destiny. I only engage in things that keep
me spiritually alert.

_____

_____

_____

_____

_____

_____

_____

_____

_____

_____

_____

51

YOU ARE UNIQUE

...that the sharing of your faith may become effective by the acknowledgment of every good thing which is in you in Christ Jesus (Philemon 1:6)

Every man's life is a bespoke gift from God. Love yours; enjoy every bit of your journey and own your story. There's a copyright license for your life. No one needs to die for you to live; No one needs to fall for you to rise. The sky is too wide for birds to collide. The diversities of God's gifts are too immense for there to be duplication and the magnanimity of God to mankind is too great for you not to be blessed.

A - Appreciate God's Times and Seasons for you
B - Be Firmly Secure in your Call and Giftings
C - Celebrate Others
D - Detest Envy and Jealousy
E - Enjoy Every BIT of YOU and Yours
F - For YOU are fearfully (full of respect and reverence) and wonderfully made.

YOU are Unique and Distinct!

Thank You Father, for making me unique. Help me to acknowledge my uniqueness and enable me to reach the great heights You have destined for me.

52

PECULIARLY FAMILIAR!

*For you did not receive the spirit of bondage again to fear, but
you received the Spirit of adoption by whom we cry out, "Abba,
Father." (Romans 8:15)*

In our relationship with God, "familiarity brings contempt" does not apply. The more we get "familiar" with Him, the more He is content with us and we are satisfied in Him. He's the only One you can absolutely open up to without the risk of being condemned. He immerses us in the ocean of His pure love in spite of our past; He's touched by our constant infirmities. He affirms us, our inadequacies notwithstanding; He's our greatest cheerleader as we journey on the path to destiny and He keeps assuring us of a hope and expected end.

What a God! What a Love! What an Access to the Most High, whom we call by name!

*Thank You my Father, for opening your arms for me to
come to You without fear. I cherish our relationship and
I long for a closer walk with You.*

_____

_____

_____

_____

_____

_____

_____

_____

_____

_____

_____

_____

53

STOMPING ON STORMS

And when the disciples saw Him walking on the sea, they were troubled...immediately Jesus spoke to them, saying, "Be of good cheer! It is I; do not be afraid."
(Matthew 14:26-27)

When the storms of life roar:

Some stir the storm the more,
Some try as much to calm the storm,
Some scream through the storm and..
Some drown in the storm....
BUT we belong to the heritage of those who
WALK on the storm!
Peter said, "If it is You Lord, bid me to come" and Jesus said to him "Come".
We are Water-Walkers; just like Jesus our Master and Role-Model!

High or Low Moments, Strong or Struggling Times, Rich or Broke Seasons, Discerning or Vulnerable Phases, Cold or Hot Weather, God never takes a break from His Role as our Father; He's not a fair-weather Friend. If He won't give up on you, there's no reason not to forge ahead.

Declaration: I will not give up until I win. I am more than a conqueror through Christ.

_____

_____

_____

_____

_____

_____

_____

_____

_____

_____

_____

_____

54

REWARDED, RESTORED

For your obedience has become known to all. Therefore I am glad on your behalf; but I want you to be wise in what is good, and simple concerning evil. (Romans 16:19)

Go and wash in the pool of Siloam, Jesus said to a blind man in John 9:7. This blind man's healing had happened right from the moment Jesus put mud on his eyes. Some other person would have felt so upset and slighted that Jesus "added salt to injury" by putting mud on his blind eyes, but off he went to Siloam; someone holding him by the hands, some others cheering him on, some following him to see what would happen and some making jest of him.

As long as you have encountered Jesus, your glorious destiny is sure, but one thing will take you there – OBEDIENCE! Celebrate your helpers, embrace the doubters, and pray for your detractors. Give ALL the glory to God when your Miracles arrive.

Lord, I receive the grace to be obedient to the instructions You give me. I will fulfill my glorious destiny in Jesus' name.

_ _

_ _

_ _

_ _

_ _

_ _

_ _

_ _

_ _

_ _

_ _

_ _

55

SMALL ERRANDS ARE NOT ERRANT
ERRANDS

He sent a man before them—Joseph—who was sold as a slave.
They hurt his feet with fetters, He was laid in irons. Until the
time that his word came to pass, The word of the Lord tested him.
(Psalm 105:17-19)

Joseph and David had something in common –
their fathers sent them on errands to go check on
their brothers and that jumpstarted their Journey to
the "Palace". The journey was long, the road was
bumpy and tumultuous; they saw hell, promises got
broken, they were betrayed, the storms of life swept
by, but they both reigned in the Palace. You never
know the "errand" that will activate your journey to
the Palace.

Stay cool headed | Don't despise little things| Honor
authority | Obey instructions | Do your tasks with
Joy | Stay focused | Forgive always |
Trust God for fulfillment.

Thank You Lord that You are with me through every turn of life's journey. I will be diligent with every assignment given to me and I will not miss the route to the palace in Jesus' name.

_____

_____

_____

_____

_____

_____

_____

_____

_____

_____

_____

_____

56

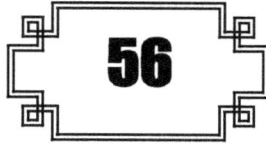

AUDITION FOR A DIVINE MISSION

But you are a chosen generation, a royal priesthood, a holy nation, His own special people, that you may proclaim the praises of Him who called you out of darkness into His marvelous light. (1 Peter 2:9)

Gone are the days when women carry calabashes (bottle gourds) and baskets on their head to go to the farm, fetching water, getting pregnant yearly and competing with a dozen other women for the attention of their husbands. God has made resources available for us to thrive and be great. He has endowed us with amazing talents and He surrounds us with those He has invested so much of his exquisite giftings into. Hand in hand, let's make the world a better place for ourselves, our families, husbands, children and our generation at large.

We are not a Calabash-on-the-head generation of women. We | Bash the devil| Lash demons| Crash challenges| Thrash rubbish| Cash in on grace| Splash kindness| Flash goodness| Look smashing| Dress dashing| We don't speak Rash words, Gnash in rage and we don't Clash with people unnecessarily. We are Beautiful in and out.

Declaration: I will not engage in activities without purpose. I will walk hand in hand with other people around me. I will do my part to be a blessing to my world.

57

LEADERS ALSO BLEED

Now David was greatly distressed, for the people spoke of stoning him, because the soul of all the people was grieved, every man for his sons and his daughters. But David strengthened himself in the Lord his God. (1 Samuel 30:6)

To what extent can we as leaders, bear the burden of those who are weak in spite of our own cares and burdens? David led four-hundred (400) distressed men who had been battered by life! When there is one problematic person around us, we are quick to complain about such a person. We whine and "pray" the person away from us because he is such a "nuisance". The love of Christ teaches us otherwise.

Sometimes, people exhibit character flaws because of the weight of life on their shoulders; just some love and yes more love and commitment can make a difference.

How did David accomplish all he did? Alone? Oh no, He had men, great men and they must have been out of those 400! Troublemakers can actually become your Bubble-makers.

Father, please help me to show unconditional love to those around me just like you love me unconditionally.

58

ADVANTAGEOUS DISADVANTAGE

*But God has chosen the foolish things of the world to put to
shame the wise, and God has chosen the weak things of the
world to put to shame the things which are mighty*
(1 Corinthians 1:27)

Moses at the burning bush gave God reasons he was the wrong person to meet Pharaoh for Israel's deliverance. His last excuse was, "...I am not eloquent". After much dialogue, God said, "I will send Aaron with you and He'll do the talking." God ALWAYS has a back-up advantage for every disadvantage life brings your way. When you see a disadvantage, press deeper and in it, you'll see "this-advantage".

"Every disappointment is a gateway to a divine appointment," somebody said. Moses fled Egypt, probably thinking he was a failure and a disappointment to himself and his world. But he didn't know that he was fleeing to the place of preparation for one of the greatest tasks God was going to accomplish for mankind. Honestly I can't fathom how God does it; but I have seen Him turn every one of my disappointments to "this-appointment". He will do the same for you!

Lord, I trust that You will turn every of my disappointment to this-appointment to the glory of Your name.

_ _

_ _

_ _

_ _

_ _

_ _

_ _

_ _

_ _

_ _

_ _

_ _

59

SUBMISSION PRECEDES COMMISSION

But I trust in the Lord Jesus to send Timothy to you shortly, that I also may be encouraged when I know your state...But you know his proven character, that as a son with his father he served with me in the gospel. (Philippians 2:19,22)

Often times, people engage the services of a guide when they are on a tour, to help them navigate relatively unknown terrain. Life could sometimes be described as a tour; a journey in which one goes around "performing" many engagements. Similarly, we need mentors in life so we don't take a wrong turn.

Jethro was pivotal for Moses' ministry in two dire moments of his life – when he fled Egypt, Jethro housed and tutored him for 40 years and also when the Israelites left Egypt, he gave Moses advice which would later elongate his life and bring order to his ministry (Exodus 18). There's someone, somewhere whom God has wired to be a guide to your journey in life. Do yourself good to identify such a person. That person might actually have the key to some of your current struggles.

Lord, help me to locate mentors that will help me in my journey of life. My steps are ordered in the right direction for divine connections.

_____

_____

_____

_____

_____

_____

_____

_____

_____

_____

_____

_____

_____

60

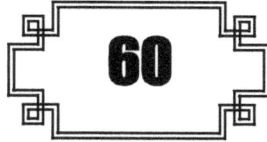

DON'T DATE THE WEIGHT

For consider Him who endured such hostility from sinners against Himself, lest you become weary and discouraged in your souls. You have not yet resisted to bloodshed, striving against sin.
(Hebrews 12:3-4)

The more you keep dating and courting your challenges, the more you become emotionally attached to them. They tend to feign importance, drain your power, keep you in pain, strain your spiritual muscles, stain your faith records, drive you in-sane and make your efforts end in vain. But if you will change your focus and date the Word of God, you will get rewards.

The Word will cause a rain of blessings, train your arms to war, break the chain of oppression, put you on a plane of success, and make you reign in life. Who would you rather date?

From today, I choose to maintain close fellowship with the word of God instead of focusing on challenges. The word of God has the final authority in my life.

_____
_____
_____
_____
_____
_____
_____
_____
_____
_____
_____
_____
_____

61

SOW; IT'LL GROW

For the earth yields crops by itself: first the blade, then the
head, after that the full grain in the head. (Mark 4:28)

As a mother, I have often wondered exactly WHEN babies grow, especially physically. A baby that could barely fill your both hands starts to increase in height and weight. Science says for kids, the most intense period of growth hormone release is shortly after the beginning of deep sleep.

No wonder God knocked Adam and Abraham into a state of deep sleep when He needed to "work" on them. When you worry much, you can't see the workings of God in and around you even when it's evident. So don't worry, remember that God is the one who brings increase. Whilst you are "waiting", SLEEP!

S: Sow (Keep sowing)
L: Learn (Never stop learning)
E: Expect (Remain Expectant of your Harvest)
E: Enjoy (Every moment in time whilst waiting)
P: Patient (Be steadfastly patient)

Lord, I rest in You. I will be not be anxious because I know You will take care of me.

_____

_____

_____

_____

_____

_____

_____

_____

_____

_____

_____

_____

62

ERROR DOESN'T MEAN TERROR

He raises the poor out of the dust, And lifts the needy out of the ash heap (Psalm 113:7)

It's usually amazing to see a baby make attempts at walking. After a few wrong, quick, timid steps, one day the baby walks and everyone is glad. Everyone in life makes mistakes. Nobody is error-proof and it is wisdom to introspect from time to time and admit our shortcomings so as not to repeat the same things that trip us over.

Oh how God loved David, the adultery and murder incidents notwithstanding. If God would count mistakes, who would stand? He won't count your mistakes, but He will make your life count instead. One can think of David's errors, but then think of God's MERCY and FORGIVENESS. If such a king could emerge from events shrouded in adultery, lies, and murder, your destiny will make sense to your generation in spite of where you have been!

Lord, I'm grateful that You look past my mistakes and flaws and in spite of them, You extend your mercy and forgiveness for a more glorious future. I receive your mercy.

63

DISRUPTED BUT NOT OBSTRUCTED

Now the birth of Jesus Christ was as follows: After His mother Mary was betrothed to Joseph, before they came together, she was found with child of the Holy Spirit
(Matthew 1:8)

Many a times, we make our plans and heaven laughs. Not because they won't come to pass, but because our desires and aspirations will come to pass in ways far beyond our imagination; good and bad, high and low, mountain and valley notwithstanding.

A virgin lady just wanted her small cute family of maybe 4 or 5 people, but heaven laughed and said, "No Mary, you are actually going to be the mother of the Messiah of the world." Call it Divine Disruption!

Thank you Lord, for the big plans You have for me.
You are able to do exceedingly, abundantly, far above
my thoughts. I anticipate Your great works in my life.

64

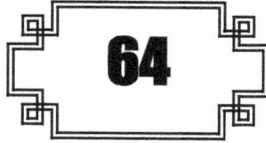

WHY ME? NOW OH ME!

Then the women said to Naomi, "Blessed be the Lord, who has not left you this day without a close relative; and may his name be famous in Israel! (Ruth 4:14)

In the school of life, if you choose to attend the class of "Why-Me?" you will constantly be taught from the board of negativity and pessimism. Life's curriculum may be very hard but a "will-succeed" and never -give-up attitude in spite of all, is a recipe for fulfillment.

Dinah was the only daughter of Jacob the Patriarch, but a demeaning rape incident sent her into permanent obscurity. Quit the "Why-Me" class; sign up for the "Oh-Me!" class instead and like Naomi, you will enjoy "Now-Oh-Me!" order of blessings! God is the Lifter of the downtrodden, through Him we soar on the wings of Grace.

Declaration: I rise from the valley of negativity and pessimism and I enroll in a higher class of possibility. I therefore enjoy God's abundant blessings.

_____

_____

_____

_____

_____

_____

_____

_____

_____

_____

_____

_____

65

A CUE FROM GOD'S CLUE

Your ears shall hear a word behind
you, saying, "This is the way, walk in it,"
Whenever you turn to the right hand
Or whenever you turn to the left (Isaiah 30:21)

David and his men's wives, children and properties had been taken captive and it was such a debilitating state that David's loyal men thought of stoning him. Everybody wept; it was chaotic and devastating. David was distressed but he encouraged himself and asked God if he could chase after the captors.

Right after he obeyed God, and started chasing, they came across a small Egyptian chap who had been left behind by his master because he was sick. He had been left sick and starving for three (3)days; yet he didn't die. You know what? That guy knew exactly where the captives had been taken to and He took David and his band right there and they recovered ALL. God always leaves a clue for us – a way out of the most unbearable circumstances.

Thank You Lord because You prepare a way for me out of every difficult situation. My eyes are open and my ears are attentive to Your leading.

_____

_____

_____

_____

_____

_____

_____

_____

_____

_____

_____

_____

66

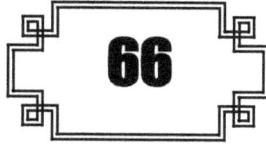

NESTED BY THE BREASTED GOD

You open Your hand
And satisfy the desire of every living thing (Psalm 145:16)

As a mother, I know how it feels to be away from a baby who is still being breastfed for so long during the day. The breasts become engorged and that comes with some uncomfortable feelings sometimes. Nature has made it so, that once it's time to feed the baby, irrespective of the distance; the mother's body begins to react.

This has made me understand this scripture better. "Can a mother forget the baby at her breast and have no compassion on the child she has borne? Though she may forget, I will not forget you!" (Isaiah 49:15). God feels our infirmities and like a nursing mother, He knows just when it's right to meet our every need. He's our Elshaddai - The Breasted God, All-Sufficient...Trust Him!

Father, I thank You for Your promise not to leave or forsake me. May this truth be my anchor through every season of life in Jesus' name.

_____
_____
_____
_____
_____
_____
_____
_____
_____
_____
_____
_____

67

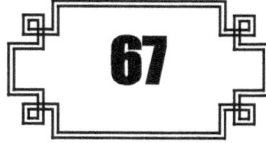

LEND A HELPING HAND

So the people asked him, saying, "What shall we do then?" He answered and said to them, "He who has two tunics, let him give to him who has none; and he who has food, let him do likewise."
(Luke 3:10-11)

May the Lord give and make us good examples of women like Puah and Shiphrah (Exodus 1:15) who by wisdom and tact stood up to defend the ethos and principles of God. Through them, generations of the children of God were preserved.

It didn't matter what the world system wanted or what a godless king dictated; they chose to fear God instead. They weren't on the pulpit, but they were fulfilling destiny right at their duty posts. No time for shenanigans, competition, envy, "biting-from-the-back", chasing ulterior motives and no receiving of bribes to keep some children alive. God gave them their own families and made them great. It's honorable to fear God above man.

Lord, help me to impact my generation for good. When others are easily enticed to lower their standards, help me to stand firm, upholding your principles.

_____

_____

_____

_____

_____

_____

_____

_____

_____

_____

_____

_____

_____

68

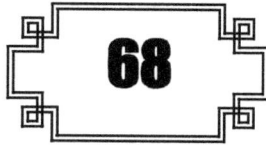

MACRO-STAGE OR MICRO-STICK

*"Most blessed among women is Jael, The wife of Heber the
Kenite; Blessed is she among women in tents.*
(Judges 5:24)

Deborah, the fierce and exuberant judge of
Israel went to the forefront of the battle with the
king. Jael the quiet, calm-natured but tactful stay-at-
home mum killed Sisera the captain of the enemy's
camp right in her house. They both were great
women who fulfilled God's agenda.

Whether extroverted or introverted, big or small,
on the pulpit or on the knees, holding a
microphone or turning the wooden stick; executive
or homemaker, known or obscure, being served or
serving others: Everyone, every woman, has a part
to play in the agenda of God. Variety is beautiful
and God in His wisdom made it so. Play your part
and celebrate others. Never look down on anyone!

Declaration: I will not look down on anyone but I will seek to celebrate the unique way God made each individual. I will work together with others to fulfill God's agenda on earth.

_____

_____

_____

_____

_____

_____

_____

_____

_____

_____

_____

_____

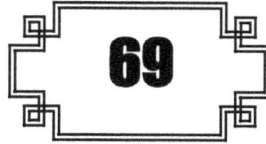

69

PAY DAY!

And He said to them, "Take heed and beware of covetousness, for one's life does not consist in the abundance of the things he possesses." (Luke 12:15)

We brought nothing into the world and we'll take nothing out of it... But wait a minute, we brought something into this world and we'll take something out of it! What makes a man is not physical things, but the abundance of endowment locked up inside him by his Maker.

From the womb through birth to childhood, teenage years and adulthood; a string of Divinely Orchestrated Events, Disappointments and Relationships unleash these hidden Potentials and "MAKE" the Man. When he leaves, he takes nothing physical out because a report sheet has gone ahead of him, summarizing all he's done whilst on earth. Whether good or wicked, our everyday deeds are the only things that matter.
Let every man live purposefully and destiny-focused. There is a Divine Pay-Day!

From today, I will live a purposeful and destiny-focused life. I will utilize my God-given abilities and accomplish all that God has in mind for me.

_____

_____

_____

_____

_____

_____

_____

_____

_____

_____

_____

_____

70

BLESSED ABOVE THE REST

Bathsheba therefore went to King Solomon, to speak to him for Adonijah. And the king rose up to meet her and bowed down to her, and sat down on his throne and had a throne set for the king's mother; so she sat at his right hand. (1 Kings 2:19)

Oh how I love Abigail! – Beautiful, Sterling qualities, Giver, Talker, Motivator, Virtuous, Supportive, Godly, 21st century kind of Celebrated woman, CNN-interviewed, Forbes-listed, Most-followed on Twitter etc...When it came to what mattered the most, Bathsheba the relatively unknown cast-aside "adulterer" produced the Crown-Prince and Heir Apparent to David's throne.

Man looks for the Best, the one with Zest, but God picks the Messed, Stressed and Depressed; Tests the Chest, puts a Vest of Mercy; Invests Grace, Bequests Favor and announces her Blessed above the Rest. Celebrate your sister, don't castigate her. Be a Lifter. You don't know what's on God's mind and on God's plate for her!

Declaration: I celebrate the uniqueness of others. I do not bring others down but I lift them up.

Other Books by the Author:

God's Choice Of The Chosen
(Co-Authored)

God's Choice of the Chosen
(7 Vs' about David) is an expository book
that explores the life and lessons of an
extraordinary Bible character called
David.

Rubies Of Wisdom

Rubies of Wisdom is a 40-Day
Devotional on Biblical Women and
Finance related issues. It offers nuggets of
wisdom to men and women alike.

To Contact Sola Adesakin:

For more information about The Author, Special Discounts about this Book and all other Inquiries, Please email:

info@fruitfoundation.org
info@smartstewards.com

Or visit:

www.smartstewards.com